Why
Buying
a Car
Sucks

and What to Do About It

By Tina – The Queen of Cars

Dedicated to the love of my life. You are my rock, my sun, my everything.

Contents

Preface

The time had finally come for me to purchase my first new car and I was very excited. My heart was set on a sporty Toyota Celica GTS. I loved it. It was very angular with a big spoiler. The car spoke to me and it said "buy me!"

I was young to be buying a car on my own but I assumed that I would be able to get a good deal on the car. I had already been negotiating and translating for my parents since I could talk, how hard could it be?

So I haggled and ended up buying my first new car and I loved it. I traded in my old car, put some money down and ended up leasing it. The payment seemed high, but she was mine!

Shortly after buying "Cinnamon" (yes I named her), I was in an accident. I was unhurt but Cinnamon was destroyed.

I bought many cars after Cinnamon, all of which I negotiated by myself too. It always seemed so difficult to negotiate a deal and every purchase left a bad taste in my mouth.

Fast forward over a decade since Cinnamon and my life was very different. I was now a successful real estate broker and owned a chain of car dealerships. I hadn't really had to negotiate a car purchase in years. A dealer gets cars very differently from the average consumer.

One day while moving some boxes, I came across the paperwork for the Celica. Out of curiosity, I pulled out the contract for the purchase. I was in shock.

I had paid roughly $15,000 extra for the car between aftermarket products, warranties and worst of all, almost $7,000 over sticker price. I felt so angry and taken advantage of.

I grew up with a deep respect for money. Both of my parents emigrated from China with nothing but an ethic of hard work. From a very young age, I knew how important money was and learned to stretch every dollar.

Seeing proof that I had given away $15,000 in one brief negotiation sickened me. Especially when I thought about how many hours my parents would have had to work to make that kind of money.

That experience is what gave me the motivation to write this book. I believe my unique perspective as both a consumer and a dealer gives me the ability to see it from both sides. I believe both sides benefit when everyone has all of the facts.

Intro

As Americans, we've always had a love affair with our cars. We name them, sing about them and even make movies about them. We dream about driving down the highway with the wind in our hair. We love the sound of a car so much that new car manufacturers pump fake engine sounds through car stereo systems that are too quiet or wimpy sounding. We love how they look, calling them sexy or beautiful. We even love their smell, especially that "new car smell". [1] In short, we can't get enough of our cars.

If owning a car is so wonderful, then why is buying one so miserable? You hear the horror stories about being ripped off. Maybe you've even experienced high pressure sales tactics or a bait and switch advertisement. Maybe you're even driving a car you no longer want just to avoid putting yourself in these situations.

Buying a car today is more jarring than ever before. In the days of Amazon, most things can be bought with just a click. Even mortgages, once phonebooks worth of paperwork, have

---

1 Hate to burst your bubble, but that new car smell is formaldehyde escaping from the plastic of a newly built car.

been reduced to online apps. To the modern consumer, negotiating for a car seems so... archaic.

These feelings lead to questions. Why do dealerships even exist? Why can't there just be one price for a car? Why is there negotiation? Why do I have to deal with a salesman?

These questions have led to businesses trying to provide solutions for consumers. AutoNation, the largest chain of auto dealerships in America, went to a no haggle price on all of its vehicles. Services, like TrueCar, give you a price you "should" pay for a car but leaves it to you to negotiate that price. Costco goes a step further and will pre-negotiate your new car for you. And my personal favorite, Carvana lets you buy your car from a giant vending machine without negotiation, oversized coins and all!

Unfortunately, these options are expensive and because of that most of these solutions either failed or have huge flaws. The no haggle way of buying cars is much more expensive. Consumers are then forced to deal with the hassle of negotiation, or to pay thousands more for the privilege of not negotiating. But it's always been that way, if you go to any car dealer in the country and say "that one" and don't negotiate, it will be pleasant.

The second problem, is that customers aren't really sure what they want. Studies have shown that 4 out of 5 customers leave with a different vehicle than they were originally looking at! But vehicle buyers have always been this way. Henry Ford famously said, "If I had asked customers what they wanted, they would have said a faster horse."

So, for the time being, you are probably going to buy your next car from a dealership. But, that doesn't have to be a bad thing. Buying from a dealership gives the consumer the ability to pay much less for a car than their neighbor did.

That small positive bit aside, AutoMD.com did a study about the car buying public. It found that most customers would rather go to the dentist than negotiate for a car. So with that uplifting statistic in mind, I'm going to share some of the funniest stories of things I've seen and experienced at car dealerships over the years at the end of every chapter. I assure you they are all true, even the hooker and the van.

This book is broken up into three main parts. The first part discusses why the car business is set up the way it is. There is a decent amount of history in this and some of it is pretty funny. It's the shortest of the three parts but really helps you understand why things have to be a certain way sometimes.

The second part is about the game plan. What you need to do, decide and research before you go to a car dealership. This is the lion's share of what's needed to get a great deal with little, if any stress.

The third part is all about buying a car today. From the pros and cons of new vs. used to the actual negotiation, it's all here.

I've also included a bonus section about buying a car with bad credit. Trying to buy a car with bad credit can be a hu-miliating experience but it doesn't have to be. I will walk you through this difficult scenario and help make it as pain free as possible. If you have or know someone with bad credit, this is a must-read.

It is my hope that by the time you have finished reading this book, you will be able to walk into any dealership and be confident that you can get a great deal.

PART 1:

How Did We Get Into This Mess?

CHAPTER 1:

Dealerships

To understand something completely you need to start at the beginning. The beginning for the dealership model starts with Hitler's favorite car guy[2], Henry Ford.

Before Ford, cars were not mass market items. They were made slowly and by hand, usually one craftsman. Those vehicles were expensive and rare. They would be sold through mail order catalogs or through roving demonstrations. This worked fine because so few cars were sold.

But with Ford's innovation of the moving assembly line, he created massive amounts of reliable and inexpensive vehicles. The problem then became getting them in the hands of the public and maintaining them.

Ford had the idea of approaching the owners of full service gas stations[3] and asking them to sell his cars. In Ford's mind,

---

2 Ford was a believer in eugenics, basically the improvement of the human population by controlled breeding to prevent undesirable heritable characteristics. Hitler claimed that Ford's book on the subject inspired his extermination of the Jews.

3 Even though Ford made vehicles a mass market item, there were already enough cars in America for a nationwide web of gas and service stations.

this was perfect. His vehicles needed to be maintained and service stations had the ability to do it. And unlike general stores, they had the room to store and explain the vehicles as well.

However, the service stations were not interested. It was too expensive and risky. They would have to buy the vehicles first and hope someone would buy them. They would also need an expensive remodel to accommodate the sales customers. And worst of all, the customers could still order directly through Ford, cutting them out of the sale after they took such a huge risk.

Ford made an agreement with the service stations that addressed their concerns. Basically, Ford would not sell their cars direct to consumers but would instead extend credit to the service stations. In return, the stations would become Ford dealerships at the owner's expense and would be responsible for selling and maintaining all Ford vehicles. Almost every car manufacturer copies this model.

Over time, disputes arose between dealers and the car makers. Some car manufacturers broke their agreements and sold direct to the consumer, others allowed competing dealers of the same brand to open practically next door.

These abuses led to basic laws protecting dealers across the country. As the dealers became wealthier and more powerful, they pushed for even more legal protections. They didn't just focus on the laws. They created powerful dealer associations with the dealer's best interest in mind.

Over the last 100 years or so, the car makers and dealers have forged an almost unbreakable bond, legally and financially.

The relationship isn't all bad though. The strong protection has allowed dealers to invest in the state of the art facilities, sometimes costing tens of millions of dollars and to be able to pay for expensive remodels to keep them that way regularly. It also allows the different car makers to sell and service their vehicles across the world with no investment.

This has all led to a situation that would make it all but impossible for a current car maker to eliminate the dealer model. Well, what about someone new? Is there a better way?

Only one new car manufacturer of note has launched in America in decades, Tesla. Tesla shocked the world with its futuristic all electric cars. Their innovation has also extended to the way they would sell cars, direct to the consumer.

The first time many Americans heard about dealer franchise laws was because of Tesla. It made nationwide news when many states would not allow them to sell directly to the consumer because of the existing franchise laws.

Tesla decided to challenge these laws but entrenched manufacturers and dealers fought them at every turn. Tesla ended up losing in most states. This has resulted in Tesla commenting publicly that they will "probably" pursue the dealer model.

What does all this mean for you? Basically, the dealer model is here to stay for quite a while. There are other alternatives popping up and we will discuss some of them in later chapters. But for now, assume your next car will be bought from a dealership.

Funny but True

I was the manager at a dealership that was launching a new ad campaign. The campaign was centered on helping people who were trading in cars with negative equity. Negative equity means that you owe more on your car than it's worth. It's also called being "upside down" on your trade.

I had a great idea to help the ad campaign. We could take a cheap trade in and flip it over at the front of the dealership. I would put a banner on it saying "Upside down? We can help!" I thought it was very clever.

I found a cheap car and had all the fluids drained and had my banner made up. It was a go!

I took all of the sales associates outside after a meeting and had them push the car to where we wanted it. It was a perfect spot, right on the edge of our property next to a highway.

We had a rope attached to the driver's door and attached the other end to a truck on the other side of the car. The salesmen helped lift the driver's side of the car while the truck pulled it. It worked like a charm, the car rolled onto its roof just like planned.

Suddenly, a Jeep pulled off the highway next to us. He wanted to know if someone needed help. We all laughed and explained what we were doing. He thought it was great and asked if could drive onto the car with his Jeep.

Blame it on the moon or endorphins from just flipping the car over, but I said yes. A few people whipped out their phones to record the Jeep drive onto the car. It was hilarious.

Then something happened. His tire somehow got wedged in the wheel well of the car and he couldn't get it out. By this time, the crowd had grown to watch the spectacle and mechanics were crawling on the car trying to figure out how to extract the Jeep.

As I'm watching this I start to feel like maybe this wasn't as clever of an idea as I first thought it was. Suddenly, we hear sirens and horns. When I look down the highway, I see a firetruck and a few police cars. The police cars block off our end of the highway while the firetruck races straight for us. More police cars show up, a couple ambulances and another firetruck. The firemen grab some tools and race to us.

I try to intercept them to explain but they rush right past me to the scene of the "accident". More police and paramedics show up, it's quickly getting out of control.

I finally talk to someone in charge and explain the situation. He was not amused. He told me that they had received multiple calls about a car accident that sounded very serious – a car upside down, the other car on top of it and a valiant effort by bystanders trying to rescue people.

Needless to say, we removed our car and ran the promotion sans prop. I still have the unused banner.

CHAPTER 2:

Why the Negotiating?

Okay, dealers are here to stay. But surely there is a better way for them to sell cars? Why is there not a set price? Why do I need a salesperson? Why do they always have to talk to their manager?

Well, it comes down to history and huge amounts of money.

Go back in time a 100 years or so and people mainly used horses for transportation. And because every horse is different, people negotiated heavily over their value. That's where the term horse-trading comes from.

As the car became more common, people started looking at replacing their horses. Early cars and horses had a lot in common from a consumer point of view.

For one, they were both expensive. Cars today are actually a lot cheaper for consumers. Both the horse and the car served as transportation, both needed maintenance and both were each unique. Early cars were hand built and just as every horse was different, so were the cars. So naturally, people wanted to buy them the same way, by negotiating a fair price.

Cars rapidly replaced horses, in a few short years actually. This left all the "horse traders" out of a job. At the same time, new dealerships desperately needed people to sell and negotiate the cars they were selling. As I'm sure you have already figured out, these two groups noticed each other quickly and just like that the modern dealership was born.

Even today, older salespeople call negotiating on a car "horse trading". So basically, you get to negotiate for your car because some horses had white spots and some didn't.

But why is there still not a set price to this day? Well, it's the consumer's fault. It turns out people still want to negotiate for their car. Hard to believe you say? Let's look at AutoNation.

AutoNation is a huge chain of new car dealerships. They are the largest dealer chain in America. It is a massive, publicly traded corporation. The CEO had been hearing for years how much people hated negotiating for cars so he made a bold move.

From now on, all vehicles would have one price and nobody would be allowed to negotiate that price. They looked at what the average person negotiated off the price of their vehicles and made that their "no hassle" price. These prices were very fair, beyond fair some said. They advertised this new policy and price structure everywhere. It blanketed the airwaves and newspapers nationwide. But there was one little problem, people stopped buying from AutoNation. No matter how much they spent, fewer and fewer customers were buying from them nationwide. This was at a time of huge increases overall in cars sale volume.

AutoNation eventually had to declare bankruptcy and revert back to the old negotiation model. They are doing fine today.

So now you're probably saying something to yourself along the lines of "fine, I have to negotiate and I have to buy at a dealership, but why do they make it so hard?" Well, it doesn't have to be. There is a saying in the car business: "It's always quicker to pay sticker." This means you can walk into any dealership, point at a car, say "That one," write a check and be out in 20 minutes. But as AutoNation proved, people need to feel like they negotiated themselves a deal.

As to why it is so difficult once you've decided you're going to negotiate… well there are a few reasons.

First, how much do you make an hour? How hard would you work to make 10 times that, what about 100 times? How much would you put up with to make $30,000 an hour? I'm guessing a lot. Considering that a 20-minute "intense" negotiation could save you $10,000, is it worth it? Of course! Well, the dealer knows this because it works the opposite way too! Just like you can save massive amounts of money on a vehicle, they can make it.

Second is the skill disparity. A good salesperson may negotiate 150 deals a month and sell 30 of them. At 150 deals a month, they are negotiating 1,800 a year. The average consumer buys a car once every 2.5 years. So each car purchase worth of experience you gain, the salesman gains 4,500 times more!

Additionally, salespeople may spend hours a day on training, go to sales training seminars and gain lessons from other salespeople, some of which have been selling for 40-50 years!

No wonder it's so hard. But the consumer has the ultimate not so secret weapon, the power to say no. This wildly levels the playing field. And you, by reading this book, gain the advantage. So to paraphrase the question: "why is negotiating so hard?" Because it's worth it.

Funny but True

One thing people don't realize is that everyone buys a car. That crazy guy talking to himself, that lady who drives a car full of kids into a river, the psycho that drives his car into a crowd. They've all bought cars.

Basically, if you're in the car business long enough, you run into all these people. Unfortunately, it's our job to sell them a vehicle. Usually you have to grin and bear it as they tell you how the president is actually controlled by an ancient powerful cabal. You ignore the racist and misogynistic comments and do your job.

One day, one of these super special customers shows up. He is a vile excuse for a human. We put up with a lot, but this guy was over the top.

I pulled the salesman aside and told him to get rid of the guy. His eyes got wide and he begged me to let him sell the guy a car. To understand his plea, you have to know a bit about pay plans. Salespeople usually get paid a "commission" for a deal and they also get bonus money for hitting certain volume goals from both the car dealer and the manufacturer.

This was the last day of the month and the combination of the commission and two bonuses would pay him almost $3,000. His wife had just lost her job and he desperately needed the money. So against my better judgment, I allowed the deal to proceed. I regretted it instantly. The customer must have sensed something changed because he came on full force. I won't repeat what was said, but the salesman was African American and this person thought it was 1842 in Alabama. That deal was probably one of the longest hours of that salesman's life. It's amazing what someone will do for his or her family. Finally, he left and we all basically forgot about the incident. Well, in Nevada anyways. After the bank finalizes the loan and the dealer processes the paperwork, a customer has to pick up a form to register the car at the DMV, including Mr. Wonderful.

We were outside listening to a band. The motorcycle dealership next door was having a fundraiser when a car comes flying into the dealership at an insane speed. It makes a turn around an island and tires squealing aims for a parking spot. He's going so fast that he doesn't notice the man on his cellphone walking across one of the spots. The car slams on its brakes and the man jumps out of the way, narrowly avoiding a tragedy.

Half of the dealership was standing outside listening to the band and we were all stunned when Mr. Wonderful jumps out of the car. He turns on the man he almost hit and starts screaming profanities at him. It was quite the sight. This little, bald chubby man is screaming at this guy twice the size of him. We realized that Mr. Wonderful thought the man was a salesman. A reasonable thought because he had a polo shirt on like the one our salesmen owned. After all, he was at a car dealership, or so he thought. He was actually at the motorcycle dealership's fundraiser. He had walked away from the event to make a phone call. The large man finished his phone call, closed his phone and put it in his pocket. He calmly took one step towards Mr. Wonderful and slapped him. It sounded like a gunshot crack! Mr. Wonderful hit the ground so fast and so hard that he bounced a bit. The misidentified salesman walked over to him and said, "I don't know who you think you're talkin' to, but I ain't him." He then walked back to the event. Mr. Wonderful had hauled himself up and was half sobbing, half gasping. He saw us all standing there and jumped back in his car and left. He never did register his new car. I have no idea how he kept driving it, but I do know that karma is a bitch.

PART 2:

Before Buying a Car

CHAPTER 1:

Start off how you want to end

Before you even go to a car dealership, you need to be prepared. Knowing what your credit looks like, your budget and what kind of car you want is a must. Don't fool yourself that you're just going to swing by the dealership and look at some cars. That's the equivalent of being on a strict diet, being hungry, and just going to look at your favorite bakery. It's not just the basics you need to decide on. Will you purchase or lease? New or used? Hybrid? Red, blue white??? You have to hammer all of the details down.

If this book teaches me how to negotiate a great deal, why is there all the homework? It comes down to power and emotions. Ever heard the saying "knowledge is power"? I think a better term is that "applied knowledge is power." What if I gave you tomorrow's lottery numbers? Would that make you rich? No! Only applying that knowledge in the form of going and buying the ticket would. So you must apply what you are going to learn. You must go through the effort of answering all the questions about your purchase before going to the dealership. Figure out what your trade is worth, know what interest rate you qualify for and don't take just anyone's word for it.

The second reason you need to do your homework before going to the dealership is emotional. There was a study done and it found that only 20% of people end up buying the vehicle they intended to. How can that be? Read any sales book and it will tell you that humans buy very irrationally. Think about our diet metaphor. How many times have you justified a snack to yourself while dieting? Does something along the lines of "well I did my full workout today, I deserve this" sound familiar?

Salespeople are trained to look for these emotional triggers. When you are walking down an unending row of beige blah-mobiles and suddenly say, "Oh, that's a nice color," the salesperson kicks into action. In the business, that simple sentence is called a "buying signal". Salespeople are trained to take a meandering course to the vehicle you say you wanted, hoping to see a buying signal. The idea being, that nobody comments on a car he or she has no interest in, even if only subconsciously, and it is true 80% of the time.

Your emotions are powerful, but to get a great deal they must be under control. Having a game plan and all the facts of the purchase at your fingertips will give you the tools to resist that temptation.

Funny but True

At one dealership I worked at, it had a large service department. Customers would pull in their vehicles to talk to a service advisor and then go into the waiting room. This dealership was in the process of being remodeled and was slightly chaotic at the time. Because of this, the cars were backed up with a line of service customers. The advisors would find out what the customer needed and direct them inside, leaving the vehicles in place.

One day, a gentleman came in with a minivan to be serviced. He went through the normal process and then went inside. As the service techs were getting through the cars, they noticed the van was missing. They asked the customer, the lot porters, everyone, but nobody knew where it was.

Eventually, they decided it was stolen and called the police. After filling out the reports, the police left and we all kind of forgot about it. A couple weeks passed by and a detective from the police department showed up. He wanted to see our security camera footage. The cops were told the first time they were there that we had cameras but nobody that was there had access to the footage.

I escorted him to the room with all of the equipment and searched for the event. I was curious myself because I hadn't seen it yet either. We found the day and time the minivan pulled up. The owner talked to the service advisor and went inside. A few moments later, the man who owned the minivan came outside and lit a cigarette. A minute or so later, we see him walk out to the street and talk to a woman walking by. This was not the best part of town and the women that walked down this road were usually hookers.

When the cop and I saw this, we both kind of nervously chuckled. We were both well aware of the women who walked the streets in front of the dealership and we both assumed he was making plans for later. What happened next shocked me. The man went back to the customer lounge and the woman headed to the van. She then got in the van and drove away!

I had a million questions but neither the detective nor the camera had answers. The officer left with a copy of the tape and a promise to call me if he ever figured things out. Well, he figured them out.

Apparently, the owner of the van had just gone through a divorce. He no longer needed or wanted the van and had been trying to trade it in because of the negative equity. Everyone kept telling him he would need a large amount of down payment to trade in the van. Because of the divorce, he had no money.

Somehow he had the bright idea of getting his vehicle stolen. Between his insurance and the GAP insurance he had purchased, his vehicle would be paid in full, allowing him to buy a new car. Inspiration struck him when he saw the woman walking by. According to that woman, he told her he would give her $100 to take the van. The details of what he said and why she would agree never came out, but whatever the conversation, she did take the van.

They found the van with the woman in it at a truck stop in Barstow, a small town between Las Vegas and California. The woman was not alone. When the police found the van she was "entertaining" a truck driver. According to the detective, she had been living in the van and turning tricks in it since it was "stolen". They arrested her and towed the van back to the dealership in Las Vegas. The detective said that the van was the most disgusting thing he had ever seen or smelled. I guess the combination of certain bodily fluids and 120-degree heat produced quite the biohazard.

The prostitute's testimony and video led to the van owner being arrested. The last I heard, he had bailed out and was driving back and forth to his court appearances.

CHAPTER 2:

You attract more flies with honey than with vinegar.

Something happens to some people when they go to a car lot. Sometimes, that something is not pretty. I've heard every foul word, phrase and racial slur under the sun. I've also heard every lie you can imagine, all from the mouths of customers.

I don't know if it's mass media, fear, hate or what, but going to a dealership can bring out the worst in people. Just like a doctor who talks to people suffering everyday, or a garbage man smelling rotting trash all day, a salesperson hears lies and foul conversations every day. All those professions become immune to such things. They have to.

When people yell at a salesperson, it doesn't help anything. Nobody likes to be treated badly. People wouldn't treat someone they were buying a house from that way, but for some reason society thinks it is okay for a car salesperson, especially a used car salesperson.

What does affect them is kindness and honesty. Now while I'm not a neutral third party in this discussion, I will say this.

Every amazing deal I've ever seen a customer get was to a nice person.

This doesn't mean going crazy with it, it just means to smile and have manners. A "please" or a "thank you" and all the things your mother taught you to do can go a long ways.

An older lady was buying a car one day, nothing special about any of it. However, during the course of the deal she found out it was the manager's birthday. The next day she came in with a few pies she baked for him and a birthday card. She felt bad that he had to work on his birthday.

The sales manager was so touched that he came into the finance office where I was working and told me to resign the deal with the numbers he had revised in the computer. He had squeezed almost $2000.00 of profit out of the deal. We told her we had found her a better approval at another bank and I resigned her. She never did realize that those were the $2000.00 pies she made.

Now, I'm not telling you to go make a pie. I'm just letting you know that if I have to sell a car cheap to hit my numbers, it's always going to the nice customer.

Funny but True

Once we sold a car to a customer with very bad credit. It was a very difficult deal, but we got her approved. When the deal went to the bank for them to verify all of the documents and to verify the loan, they found a problem. The pay stubs were not real.

The customer had manufactured fake pay stubs to show where she supposedly worked. I'm sad to say we get these often and we almost always catch them. Somehow this one fell through the cracks.

I had already talked to the repo man when she showed up. We had been calling her to pick up her registration paperwork and she had come in to get it. I told her that the bank had told us that her pay stubs were fake, and we had to take the car back. She immediately jumped up and bolted out of the door. She ran to the car and jumped inside it.

It wasn't our first rodeo and had already pulled a large truck behind it to box her in. She started yelling at us to move the truck. When she realized we would do no such thing, she locked the doors and made a phone call.

As soon as the call was over, she started assaulting herself. She hit herself, scratched up her face and banged her head against the steering wheel. I have to hand it to her; she really kicked the crap out of herself. I doubt many people could beat themselves up half as well, she was a pro.

This went on for a few minutes. We couldn't turn away. It was like looking at a bad car accident. Finally, she decided that she had enough, and the beating stopped. Right after she had declared victory over her foe, the police showed up. For those not in the know, police at car dealerships is not an uncommon sight.

She had called the police and said that we were beating her and trying to steal her car. A quick review of our surveillance tapes proved otherwise.

The cops arrested her and we got our car back. Now when we tell customers news like this, we have to make some reason up to get the keys first.

CHAPTER 3:

Advertising

Advertising is what makes you buy from Billy's Chevrolet instead of Bob's Chevrolet. It's why you buy the Toyota instead of the Nissan. It's also why you buy on Memorial Day weekend[4] instead of the Tuesday before.

The problem with all these ads is that at least 75% are B.S. We have been trained as consumers to jump on deals. Black Friday, the grocery store circular in the Sunday paper and the closeouts from stores going out of business are a few examples.

You'll need to understand how most advertising works. For the most part, price based advertising works on a loss leader concept. That means the only reason your grocery store is advertising bananas at 12 cents a bunch and the electronic store is selling a 90-inch big screen for $200.00, is as bait. They advertise enticing products at a price below their cost to bring you in. They know that if you show up to buy the bananas, you're probably also going to buy other things.

---

4 Memorial Day weekend is typically the busiest car sales weekend of the year.

For vehicle sales, this concept doesn't work well. Nobody comes in to buy a Chevrolet Malibu and picks up a few Tahoes while they're at it. Dealers and manufacturers had to adapt.

Advertising for car dealers (new, franchised stores) is broken into 3 categories. They are known as Tier 1, 2, and 3. Basically, Tier 1 is "Buy a Toyota," Tier 2 is "Buy a Toyota now," and Tier 3 is "Buy a Toyota from Bob's Toyota."

Tier 1 is a brand created at the national level. For example, any time you see a commercial bragging about initial quality or winning some award.

Tier 2 is regional. The dealers have an amount on every car sold that goes to an advertising account, which is even seen on an invoice. This pool is then used to convince a customer that now is the time to buy. You see ads like "Toyota sell-a-thon," or the "spring sales event" etc.

Individual car dealers make Tier 3 advertisements. It will always reference only one dealership. A newspaper ad would be an example of a Tier 3 ad.

It's important to understand the difference, because the Tier 3 ads are usually the ones with the most B.S. in them. They might not be outright lies as they are still legal, but they will almost be impossible deals to make.

For example, let's say you are buying a new Hyundai Sonata. You have looked around a bit online and the one you want is the Limited Hybrid edition. You see them for around

$28,000. Then flipping through the Sunday newspaper, you see this advertisement.

It's a picture of a shiny Sonata for $19,875. What a deal, right? Well, not so fast. There are a few things you need to look at closer.

First is the picture. It is a picture of a Limited, but it's really a stock photo of a base model hybrid. A stock photo is used often in car advertising. It means that it is not the actual car for sale.

The other thing to notice with the price is the stock numbers in the bottom of the ad. To advertise like this, they have to include the stock number it is based on. The stripped down work truck may still cost $28,000. So for the sake of the ad, they will discount the one referenced in the stock number to $25,000.

What about the other $8,180 in discounts? That is the fine print. Typically, they are counting all rebates the carmaker offers such as owner loyalty, (owning a current Ford) trading in a current competitor's vehicle, recent college graduate active military, amongst others. The odds of having all of them are very small.

The last thing is the payment. It's based on a very favorable lease. Perfect credit, super low miles, all the rebates shown above, a large down payment and no taxes added in. This real lease would probably be double this number.

So how do you know what ads are real and which ones to ignore? The advice I give is to go directly to the manufacturer's website. All rebates, special interest rates and lease specials are listed there. I would then ignore all of the others. Any discounts or prices now bestowed at the national lever are flexible at best.

Funny but true

We had a female customer once who bought a white Dodge Ram pickup. It was a fully loaded gorgeous truck, big and shiny. About two months after she bought the truck, she came in and wanted to return it. We told her that it was impossible and she wasn't pleased.

The reality of the situation is that once the bank "funds" the deal or pays the dealer for the loan, it becomes difficult to undo the purchase and once the customer starts making payments, it's all but impossible. After realizing that we would not unwind the deal (we even told her that we had sold her trade in at the auction over a month ago), she left very angry. She stormed out and marched back to her truck. She went right up to her passenger door and kicked it, leaving a dark large dent. She then kicked it again and again. When she was satisfied, she took out her phone and took a picture. She then proceeded to walk around the vehicle kicking huge dents in it and photographing it.

We were all gathered around the security camera monitors, [5] wondering what she was thinking. It was kind of funny at first and then slowly slid to sad and creepy. After about 15 minutes of self-inflicted mayhem, she finally got into her truck. She started it up but didn't go anywhere.

---

5 I have no idea why customers don't realize that every dealership has tons of good cameras. You know Best Buy has them and they are protecting $200 TVs that are locked up at night. Car dealers have millions of dollars outside all night. Of course they would all have cameras!

After 30 minutes, a cop[6] car pulls up. She jumps out of the truck and goes to the officer. After a couple of minutes of pointing to the truck and then the dealership, the cop heads inside. We were told that she had called the police after noticing we had vandalized her truck. She stated to the officer that she had no idea why we would do such a thing. After a good laugh, we show the officer the surveillance video. In our defense, he laughed too. She was then forced to leave by the officer. To this day, I have no idea what she was trying to accomplish.

_____

6 Cops and car dealerships are another common theme. As an FYI, unless you're being assaulted or some such thing, all contract law becomes a civil dispute which cops could care less about.

CHAPTER 4:

New vs. Used

This is a question that bounces around quite frequently. Is it better to buy used or new? Well, it depends. One thing for sure is that you need to know the answer to this question <u>before</u> you go to a dealership.

Many people lean towards the new car. It's all shiny and... new. It has the new car smell and who wants to buy someone else's problems, right?

Others are die hard used car buyers. Why be a sucker and buy a new car that depreciates 20% the second you drive it off the lot?

Well, both opinions are right and both are wrong. There are good arguments for both sides, but there is usually a better choice. Let's look at the pros and cons of both.

New Cars Pros

A major pro is choice. There is no used car factory but there is a new car one. You want that Porsche in red with the optional hand painted center caps? No problem. Colors, options, trim levels and any variation you can think of that the dealer has is available.

Another huge plus is the warranty. A lot of people don't realize that some of a new car's warranty doesn't transfer. For example, Hyundai has a 5-year 60,000 bumper-to-bumper warranty and a 10-year 100,000 mile powertrain warranty *for the original owner.* Buy the same car used and it drops to the 5-year 60,000 mile warranty only.

Rebates and special interest rates usually come with a new car purchase as well. Sometimes you can even get 0% APR. The obvious pro is that it is new- new tires, new brakes, new everything. For some people, the conversation ends here.

A car depreciates massively once you buy it. Some people think it's a scam but it's not. Once you buy a car, it becomes used. New cars don't have titles. They have MSO's. The title is generated by the state you buy the car in and usually the full warranty only goes to the first owner. So even if you trade in your car after 1 month, it has lost real value. How much of a discount is a car with 1,000 miles and half of the warranty vs. a car with 0 miles and a full one- about 20% less.

New Car Cons

There really is one con to buying a new car, but it's a doozy. That con is obviously price. A new car will typically cost you more than a used car. In cases, where it's an exceptionally quickly depreci-ating vehicle, like a luxury sedan, maybe tens of thousands more.

Used Car Pros

Used cars really have one thing going for them, cost. Consid-ering how important this factor is for most people, it's easy to see why so many people buy used. It is very possible to buy a car the same model year of a new one and pay thousands less. When you're looking at a $529 payment for a new Camry and the dealer shows you the same car but the payment will be $398, it's a strong argument.

Used Car Cons

Honestly, there are very few. Buying a lightly used car versus a new car has very few drawbacks contrary to popular belief, even when it comes to the warranty and reliability. How can a used car be more reliable? Well, even new cars have mechanical issues.

You know the J.D. Power awards everybody brags about winning? Well, one of the most prestigious is the initial quality award. For years, Lexus was the undisputed leader with a score of 11. What does the 11 refer to? It's the number of mechanical issues per 1,000 vehicles.

Cars are the most advanced things most consumers will ever own, much more advanced than your smartphone or jet. These vehicles have thousands and thousands of parts manufactured all over the world in them. So having a vehicle with only 11 issues per 1000 made is something to be proud of.

If you buy a used car that is one year old, usually those issues have been ironed out by then and recalls have been made etc. This leads to a car actually becoming more reliable as a used vehicle. Over time this will change, but initially it's true.

The other perceived negative is the warranty issue. With the advent of Certified Pre-owned programs, that has largely been handled. Car manufacturers have programs that will reinstate the full factory warranty, sometimes extending it and will provide new car finance rates. These CPO's as they're called, take away most of the negatives of buying a car.

The only real drawbacks are choice and ego. You are stuck, as far as options and colors go to what is for sale. You really need to weigh how important these options are to you versus the loss of price savings. If you're reading this book, I can guess what you will choose.

As far as ego goes, if you "need" a new car then go for it. To paraphrase a popular sales guru, [7] "salesmen who sell customers what they need instead of what they want have skinny kids."

So which one do you buy?

Again, it depends. For argument's sake, let's say you only wanted the best deal possible. In most cases, you would buy used. Why most and not all? Well, at certain times, new cars can actually be cheaper than used, like at the end of the model year when the new car is showing up, especially when the new model has a different body style. The rebates and discounts can go into thousands even ten thousands on higher priced vehicles.

Another time is during a lease. We won't get into too much detail here because I'll devote a chapter to them later, but a big benefit to a lease is the ability for a business owner to write off the cost of the vehicle. While the vehicle would cost more, the net cost could be less.

Whichever you choose, for whatever reason, I will walk you through getting the best deal regardless.

---

7 Zig Ziggler said that "timid salesmen have skinny kids" but in my experience this is true for salesmen that try to sell a car based on a customer's stated needs. They sell lots of red sports cars for a reason.

Funny but true

I had a short stint working at a Bentley dealer. It was a very hard job because of how long it took to sell a car. You might talk to a customer for months only to find out they bought a Rolls Royce[8].

One customer I had been working with was a local attorney. He was semi-famous and had a catchy ambulance chaser ad playing on the TV all day every day. He came in with his girlfriend and we go on a test drive in a dark blue Bentley.

He drove the car with his girlfriend in the passenger seat and I was sitting in the middle. This particular car was close to $350,000.00. When we left the lot, it started out with the usual test drive banter. While he was asking questions about the car, his girlfriend was quietly but earnestly picking her nose. She was really going to town and was a full knuckle deep!

He kept talking but I couldn't help but stare at her mining operation. After a couple of minutes, she struck gold. She pulled her finger out and huge green and red booger came out with it. To my horror, she slowly lowered her hand to the seat and proceeded to wipe the booger across the left seat bolster[9]. I gasped out loud.

The driver looks down and sees what happened and freaks

---

8 First world problems

9 FYI, a mechanic sat in the seats of a car once with a tool in his back pocket that tore the seat. The seat cover alone was $3,000 not counting the labor to put it on

out. He starts calling her every name in the book... but with a weird twist. He called her a nasty booger bitch, a booger whore, etc. Trust me, it was much more vulgar than I'm willing to put here.

We turn around and head back to the dealership and his tirade continues but at a lower volume, almost a mumble. "Yeah, you're my nasty booger girl, aren't you?" It really started getting creepy. The conversation turned more sexual for lack of a better term.

I'm completely freaked out and texting anyone and everyone I know that I might be kidnapped into some weird booger cult. We get back to the dealership and Mr. and Mrs. Booger quickly leave. The detailer was able to clean the seats and apparently it was all over... or was it? Mr. and Mrs. Booger came back that night but that will have to wait until the next chapter.

CHAPTER 5:

To trade or not to trade...

That is the question I get most often. Should I trade it in or sell it myself? How do I get the most for my trade? Do I fix the dent in the door? All are variations of the same question, "How do I maximize my trade value?"

Sell It Yourself

First, let's look at selling it yourself. For some vehicles and some people, this is by far the best choice. If you have the right car, have the time and are comfortable dealing with strangers, you will usually come out ahead.

That's great, but there are a lot of ifs and buts. One is your car. Certain vehicles, like cars under $5,000 and specialty vehicles (think Viper or Camaro SS) are much easier to sell. The price matters because cheaper cars of all makes are always in demand and don't require financing. The uniqueness of the vehicle matters because people who want a Viper will actively seek out that vehicle where people buying an Accord usually just want reliable transportation and are rarely looking for something super specific. Even if they are, Dodge made 0 vipers and Honda made over 300,000 Accords last year. The supply of used Vipers being so low will mean that it is always an easier sale.

Second, you need time. You need time to clean it, list it, and time for it to sell. Also, don't forget the time between when you sell your car and buy another one. Do you have another car to drive? Do you have to rent one?

Let's assume the answer to every question is a yes and you want to sell the car yourself. Now let's talk about how to get the most money for it.

One of the biggest mistakes I think people make when selling private party is for the car to need mechanical or body work. A check engine light, A/C not working or a huge scratch will turn off a prospective buyer. Even if they do want to buy it, they will use these things, and rightly so, to drive the price down. Your vehicle needs to be in good shape and detailed to maximize the money you get for it.

Another mistake is bad photos. After you clean your car, take it to a nice location and take some good picture of it. People are very visual and a good picture can make all the difference.

Once you have a few good pictures and the car is ready for sale, you need to tell people. Put a for sale sign in your car. Your neighbors will be a great source to sell your car. Beyond that, you need to list your car online. Online classified sites like Craigslist, Let Go and Offerup are usually the best. If you have a more unique car, Ebay, Bring a Trailer and AutoTrader are good choices.

One word of caution, scammers are everywhere. Most scams come in the form of someone far away (a parent in another country or a serviceman deployed, etc.) buying a car for someone. They will wire you too much money by "accident" and then ask you to wire the difference back. After you do so, the first wire bounces.

If you do take a wire, cashier's check or personal check, make them wait a full 2 weeks before giving them the title or the car. If they have an issue with that, remind them that "cash is king".

Trade it in

For the majority of people, they will just trade in their car. It's easier, simpler and sometimes the only real option. In some cases, you may still have a loan on the car with negative equity or you have a brown, stick-shift, diesel station wagon that nobody but you can really appreciate.

One of the easiest things you can do is clean your vehicle well. Most people don't and most dealers assume, based on decades of experience, that a clean car is a well taken care of car.

What you shouldn't do is fix any mechanical or cosmetic issues with the car. Unlike selling to a private party, these issues won't stop you from selling the vehicle to a dealer. Not only that, a dealer can fix these issues for pennies on the dollar compared to you. So save your money. However, you should know what your car is worth so you know what a fair price is.

Many people will go to Kelley Blue Book for this. That is a mistake. Kelley Blue Book cannot give you the real value of your car because they make their money by selling this information to a dealer (they currently charge $1,600 a year, per user!) They will give other numbers that mean nothing instead.

The numbers the dealer goes off of are Kelley Blue Book lending value (which a consumer has no access to) and the auction value (given to the dealers on various auction sites, also not available to consumers). Wholesale lending value is the number the banks will lend off of and the auction price is what the car will bring at auction.

A dealer typically needs to buy a car $1-2,000 below wholesale book value, which coincidentally happens to be auction price. They need this margin to be able to repair, detail, market and sell the car.

Kelley Blue Book will give you a trade in value. I have no idea where they get that number, but after tens of thousands of deals, I've never seen it be accurate. It is usually high by about 20%. So for a quick rule of thumb, you can estimate about 20% of the trade in value on KBB.com. This is Kelley Blue Book's site for consumers.

Another thing you can do is ask your dealer for the Kelley wholesale book value and they will gladly print it out for you. It's very simple, here is an example on the next page.

Stock #: 4015
Jun 17, 2019

Retail BreakDown

Kelley Blue Book

06/14/2019 - 06/20/2019

2016 Ford Focus SE Sedan 4D	$12,120

VIN: 1FADP3F29GL282497

4-Cyl, Flex Fuel, 2.0L.. $0
Auto, 6-Spd Powershift.. $0
FWD.. $0

Equipment

Sport Pkg...............................	$204	Premium Sound....................	$94
Traction Control...................	$0	SiriusXM Satellite...............	$0
AdvanceTrac...........................	$0	Bluetooth Wireless..............	$0
ABS (4-Wheel).......................	$0	SYNC....................................	$0
Alarm System........................	$0	Parking Sensors....................	Included
Keyless Entry........................	$0	Backup Camera....................	Included
Air Conditioning...................	$0	Dual Air Bags.......................	$0
Power Windows.....................	$0	Side Air Bags.......................	$0
Power Door Locks................	$0	F&R Head Curtain Air Bag	$0
Cruise Control......................	$0	Knee Air Bags......................	$0
Power Steering......................	$0	Rear Spoiler..........................	$75
Tilt & Telescoping Wheel....	$0	No Alloy Wheels...................	($69)
AM/FM Stereo.......................	$0	Premium Wheels 19"+........	$306
CD/MP3 (Single Disc)..........	Included		

Total Value without mileage......................................	$12,730
Mileage adjustment (43217) miles...........................	$165
*** Total Wholesale/Retail Value.................................	$12,895

Auto Mart LLC
6049 Boulder Hwy, Las Vegas, NV 89122
(702) 551-3003

In this example, the car is a 2016 Ford Focus with 43,217 miles on it. The dealer inputs the VIN (vehicle identification number) and the miles and the value is shown. They will then check the appropriate option boxes based on what the vehicle has. This will give them the wholesale value.

They will then inspect your car and subtract any repairs or maintenance needed. Finally, they will subtract the margin they need from that number.

Let's assume the example above is in excellent shape but needs 4 new tires. The dealer will figure out the vehicle's value as follows:

2016 Ford Focus, 43,217 miles

$12,895 wholesale value -$400 tires = $12,495 net wholesale

- $2,000 margin = $10,495 value for trade

This will be your trade's value, give or take a few dollars, at almost every dealership you go to. This would also be the price the dealer would roughly pay if the car was purchased at an auction.

Some consumers believe they can negotiate this number, but in reality you can't. When you negotiate more for your trade-in, you are just removing profit on the deal from other areas. Internally, the dealership will own the car for the $10,495.

1) New car $25,000 – $0 no trade = $1,500 profit

2) New car $25,000- $7,500 trade = $1,500 profit

3) New car $25,000- $8,000 trade = $1,000 profit

In figure 1, you see that a given car sold for $25,000 makes the dealer $1,500. In figure 2, we add our trade and it's worth $7,500 and the customer is given $7,500, so it still makes $1,500. In figure 3, the customer negotiates this trade to $8,000. Since, the dealer still has to buy the car at its $7,500 value; they then make $500 less for $1,000 in profit.

We will go more in depth in the negotiation section. Just know it is always to your advantage to know your car's real value before negotiating.

Funny but True

In our previous funny but true story, I told you about Mr. and Mrs. Booger. What happened later was quite interesting.

By the time my weird test drive was over, it was basically time to go home. When I came in the next day, I saw everyone standing around a bright yellow Hummer. I went over to see what the excitement was about.

The hood of the Hummer was all dented up and the plastic vents on the hood were smashed. It appeared that someone had vandalized the cars. A few of us went to check out the security cameras. We looked back through the previous night to see what happened.

There they were, Mr. and Mrs. Booger had shown back up to the dealership about 15 minutes after everyone had left for the night. They meandered through the lot until they got to the yellow Hummer.

Next thing you know, he lifts her onto the hood[10] and climbs on board himself. They immediately proceed to enact several positions out of the Kama Sutra. After about 30 minutes, they got up and left the dealership.

Well, we were less shocked than you might think. After a while, you kind of get the shock burned out of you in this business. But the question remained... what should we do?

---

10 The hood on a H1 hummer is roughly the shape and size of a queen bed.

You would think we would automatically call the police, but he had just placed a deposit on a new Bentley[11]. We figured the hood on the Hummer could be fixed for about $1,500, while we were making about $40,000 on the Bentley sale.

At the end of the day, pragmatism won. With that much profit secured, we could let a hummer on the Hummer pass.

---

11 Bentleys are hand built in England to the customer's specifications, and it can take a couple months to get one built.

CHAPTER 6:

Myths

There are some pieces of advice I've seen used in all kinds of articles on how to save money buying a car. Some are okay, most are bunk. There are also things customers do or ask for no reason other than thinking they should. I'm going to go over a few myths so you can start with a clean slate when you head to the dealership.

Myth #1: Buy a car on the last day of the month for the best deal

The basis of this theory is that salespeople need to hit a certain number and by waiting to the last minute, you can use their desperation to get an otherwise unobtainable deal.

There is just enough truth in this to be plausible but it usually isn't true. The reality is that while the salesperson may need just one more deal for a bonus, that fact doesn't motivate the dealer to discount a car any more than usual.

With that being said, the dealership itself may have a goal to hit for extra money from the factory, but rarely will one deal ever make a difference. By the last week of the month, they already know if they will make the goal or not. So your last day gambit will fall on deaf ears.

Even worse for you, the dealer perpetuates these myths, which results in the last week of the month always being busier. That means the showrooms are crowded and you are even less likely to get a deal.

Myth #2: Save your trade until the last minute

I've seen this myth suggested in newspapers and even on the news. It won't save you any money but boy does it work to piss a lot of people off.

The idea is this. You negotiate the best deal possible and then at the 11th hour, you throw in your trade and expect big buck savings. Here's what really happens. As you saw in the chapter on trade-ins, there is only a certain amount of profit in a deal and your trade is worth a fixed amount of money. So when you negotiate a deal, then throw in a trade, you have negotiated out some or even most of the profit. Throwing in a trade at the last minute itself isn't a problem, but throwing one in that you owe more on than it is worth is. Or just as common, wanting more than the car is worth.

You paint the dealer in to a corner. Most of the time, it just kills the deal after an hour of work.

Myth #3: "I'm losing money on this deal"

I've had a lot of people ask me about this, and I've also heard it said a lot over the years. It is only a partial myth.

It usually goes something like this. After a tough back and forth, an exasperated dealer throws his hands up and says, "I'm already losing money on this deal!" Is this true?

Well, we've already discussed that dealers will have a certain monthly goal. If they hit that goal, they get something called hold-back or stair step money. Let's say the goal is to sell 300 units and the stair step money is $1,000 per car. That means if the dealer hits his goal he will get a bonus from the factory of $300,000.

Certain deals aren't able to be made, such as customers who are trading cars with a lot of negative equity, but the dealer can then take a loss on a deal to help them make their goal of 300 cars. However, this is rare and can almost never be negotiated. It's more of a tool of last resort to catch an extra deal that couldn't be made otherwise.

Another way is when you are buying a used car. The car could have had mechanical issues that cost more than they thought. Or it could be an old unit that the blue book has gone down on. These examples aside, I'd say a solid 75% of the time, it's B.S.

Myth #4: Play Dealer A against Dealer B

This one works like so. You go to dealer A and get their best price. You then go to dealer B and say "Dealer A said I could buy this for x amount." Dealer B then gives you a lower price and you go back to Dealer A to do the same thing.

While this one sounds good in theory, reality gets a bit messy. The reality is that the car business is a very small world.

What usually happens is that you say Dealer A gave you a certain price. The manager probably knows someone at the competing store and calls them. Many times "competing" stores are actually owned by the same person. If that's the case, the manager definitely knows someone there.

They will then get all the terms that you negotiated, the fact that you had a trade and what car you were on[12] at the other lot. Now both dealers will have a complete picture of the deal and all information necessary to negotiate the deal well.

While this isn't a myth per se, there are much less annoying and easier ways to get a good deal. Don't worry, we'll cover them.

Myth #5: Kicking tires

I have no idea where or why actually kicking a tire started, but stop.

---

12 "On" is dealer slang to represent the vehicle the customer is dealing with. She is on the blue Mazda 6, etc.

Funny but True

In the 2010's, I worked at an economy car dealer. The car manufacturer was on a high after a good string of successful vehicle launches. It got even better for them when Toyota's unintended acceleration fiasco happened. This led them to become a bit big for their britches.

In their home country, they sold a vehicle that was very expensive. It was a cross between a Rolls Royce and an S-class Mercedes. It even had the requisite champagne glasses and fridge in the back.

For some unknown reason, they decided to bring this car to America. We were to sell this beast for $80,000. It was actually quite the deal, but our customers were buying cars ranging from $12,000 to maybe $30,000.

We were forced to remodel the showroom and buy $80,000 worth of specialty tools just to work on the vehicle. The manufacturer also required us to order at least 3 of these, which we did.

Needless to say, this car was a tremendous belly flop. We only sold 2 of the 3 within a year. Considering we sold 400-500 cars a month, this is laughingly pitiful.

The last one we had was the most expensive of the three, the "el Presidente" or some such thing. It had rear seat navigation, foot rests and the ever practical champagne fridge.

The only reason we had sold the other two was because that car maker had given us $10,000 dealer cash[13] and a $10,000 rebate. To add insult to injury, the cars would also be one model year old, further reducing their value.

Two days before the rebates expired, a customer came in specifically looking for this beast. It was a miracle. They had just come from a different dealership with a price on the base model of this car. The base model was almost $18,000 cheaper.

Seeing a way out of this nightmare, I decided to talk to the customers myself. I explained our situation and offered them the deal of a lifetime. Not only would I beat the deal they had negotiated across town, I'd beat it by $5,000 and instead of them getting the base model, they would get the $18,000 more expensive el president! I could see the shock and excitement on their face.

We were actually going to lose $7,000 on the deal but in my mind it was better than trying to sell the car without the $20,000 dealer assistance money. To give you a better understanding of how good of a deal this really is, we were selling a brand new car that stickered for $90,000 for $55,000. It was literally the best deal I've ever seen.

The customer[14] gave me a sly look and said, "we'll take it for $45,000 out the door[15]. I was shocked. They genuinely

---

13 Basically a rebate to the dealer to allow them to heavily discount a car

14 There were actually two people involved, a husband and wife, but the wife (as usual) was the shot caller.

15 Out the door means all fees and taxes included.

knew what a good deal it was and asked me to go $14,000 below that!

I decided I'd rather keep the car. I told them my offer was the best we would do and they would be insane to pass it up. They continued trying to negotiate even lower with the salesman. I told him that I didn't want to hear about the deal again unless they were paying $55,000. They ended up leaving and not buying the car. They told the salesman that maybe we would reconsider their offer tomorrow (the last day of the dealer money).

After they left, their salesman came to me. He wondered if I would let him buy the car for his wife for the same price. This would usually be a hard no. Any manager losing money selling to an employee is heading for the chopping block. But, this was a special case. I said yes.

His wife came in that night. They were ecstatic, she even cried. I was just happy I had rid myself of the albatross that had been on my neck. Even the owner was happy. Losing $7,000 isn't that bad when you thought you were going to lose $20,000.

The next day the salesman came into my office with a problem. The customer had called back first thing in the morning and offered $48,000. While it was $3,000 more than the night before, it was still $11,000 less than my best price. The salesman then informed them that the conversation was moot and that the car had been sold to him[16].

---

16 In hindsight, I wished he wouldn't have shared that little tidbit

The customer was livid and came directly to the dealership. They wanted to talk to me and stormed into my office. "How could you?!" They claimed that I knew they were coming in to buy the car today. I corrected them, as they had said I might look more kindly on their insulting offer today.

Regardless, they claimed it was their car and they wanted it! As if succumbing to my high pressure they huffily claimed that they would pay the $55,000. I told them it was impossible and the car was already sold. "So get the car back! He's only a salesman," she said. That second sentence was the beginning of the end. Salespeople have to take a lot of crap. I, on the other hand, do not.

I told them the deal was final, sorry. She responded with "I'll pay $57,000." That was $2,000 more than what I offered to sell it for. But again, the car was sold. She whined, "But why can't you just take the car back?" I replied, "Because I'm not a monster. I will not take back a husband's gift to his wife." She then called me a bitch.

They left soon after, but they were the Christmas gift that kept on giving. Bad reviews online, complaints to corporate, BBB complaints and even a complaint to our local news station "Consumer Advocate".

I don't know if they ever bought a car, but I do know the salesman's wife still loves her car.

PART 3:

The Deal

CHAPTER 1:

Your Goal

At this point, you should have made all of your major decisions: the kind of vehicle, new or used, whether or not you will trade in a car, etc. But before we head to the dealership, you need to have your goals solidified. It's not good enough to just say that you want a "deal," you need a number to quantify that deal.

Besides your trade, (if you have one) there are 2 other things you need to get a number for. One is the price you're willing to pay for your vehicle, new or used. Second is the interest rate you qualify for.

New Car Price

A new car is easier to get a target price on than a used vehicle. That is because all new cars come with invoices. Invoices are like receipts for the dealer showing what was paid for the car. This single document shows you a ton of information.

There are many spots online to get the invoice to any new car you are looking at. I personally like Edmunds.com. Once you put in all of the options, you will get the invoice price. Even more simply, you can just ask the dealer. Dealers would rather deal with an informed buyer rather than someone negotiating from a place of ignorance. One can be made into a deal, the other can't.

The invoice will look something like this document below, however every manufacturer is slightly different.

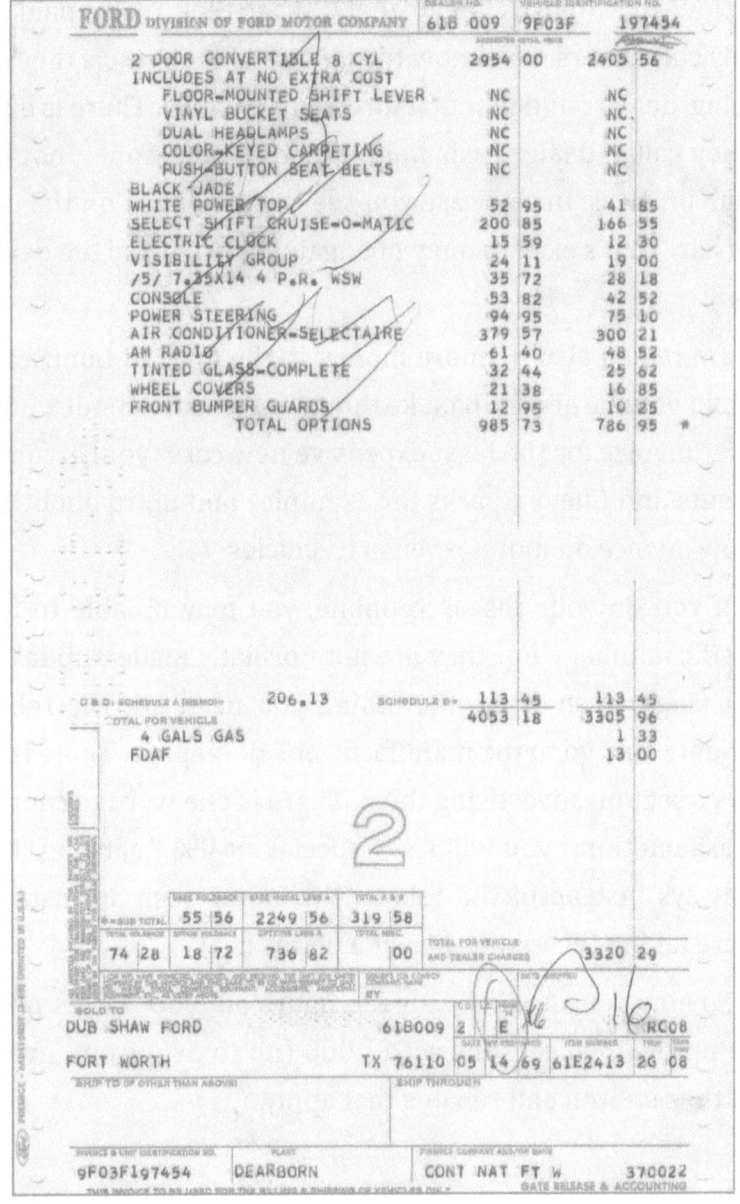

Sorry for the example (it's from 1969) but car manufactures aren't that keen on me sharing a new invoice apparently. But it's the exact same. The bottom invoice number is what you need to pay attention to. That number is the dealer's "cost".

Now that doesn't mean that's what they really paid. So many consumers now know the invoice of the vehicle they are buying, dealers and manufacturers got creative. There is extra money called dealer cash, hold back or trunk money, not put in the invoices. In this case you see the hold back on the bottom left. That's extra money not against the invoice the dealer has.

There can also be more money in the form of bonuses at certain volume goals. To make things easy, figure about $1,000 under invoice for the least expensive new cars (your Hyundai Accents and Chevy Sparks for example) and up to about 5% below invoice on more expensive vehicles.

If you do your research online, you may be able to find specific numbers, but they are not normally made public and do change often. The other thing you need are the rebate amounts. Just go to the manufacturer's homepage. There is always a section advertising them. There is one word of caution here. Sometimes you will see a special for 0% financing. This is always instead of the rebate. I've never seen an instance where taking the rebate wasn't a better deal.

So now you should be able to figure out your target price. Pull up the invoice, subtract $1,000 (up to 5%) from invoice and then subtract all rebates that apply.

Used Car Price

The best price on a used car is a bit of a moving target. Basically, there is no way to know what a dealer paid for it. But it doesn't matter; a good price for you has no bearing on what they paid for it.

Your online research tools are limited. You can look at what other people are selling the same car for, but that only shows their asking price, not the price someone could negotiate.

The only way it would be better is if you had a high interest rate, but it's a moot point because you need great credit to qualify for a 0% rate anyway.

Kelley Blue Book is as useless to the consumer as ever. Every dealership, bank, credit union, auction, divorce lawyer and payday loan place on earth pays Kelley $700 a year per user, not per business but per person. If they gave away information online that was even reasonably accurate, they would lose billions in subscription fees.

Your best source again is the dealers themselves. Just ask to see the retail and wholesale book sheet. Most will give it to you and if they won't, take your business elsewhere.

So, how much do you pay? There is no set number because every used car is different, but retail book value is what they should be asking for the car, wholesale book value is what they should own it for after all repairs, detail, marketing etc. The closer to wholesale you can get, the better.

Financing

You're almost always better off allowing the dealer to arrange financing. They have access to dozens of banks and the rates are usually lower. Plus, it's less hassle for you.

However, just because they are arranging it, doesn't mean you don't have a say in it. A dealer can work up your interest rate by 2 or 3 percentage points. Both the bank and the dealer pocket those profits.

Your best bet is to poke around online and look for a low rate. Look at your bank and at a few local credit unions. The lowest of these becomes your target rate. The dealer can then match your rate[17] or you can go yourself and get the lower rate.

You now have all of the information you need. It's time to go buy a car!

---

17 The dealer will match this rate 95% of the time. Even if it's the same rate, they still pocket a small flat bonus fee from the bank.

Funny but true

Anytime you go on a test drive, there is a process the sales-man is supposed to follow. The main part of this process is copying the customer's driver's license. This is a requirement for the insurance companies, and it verifies that you actually have a license[18]. It also verifies that you are 18 years of age[19] and it is a record if the car gets stolen[20]. These are all import-ant details for our story.

One day a beautiful young woman came in looking for a car. One of our younger salesmen upped her. It was a good match; you could tell they had hit it off. He walked her around the dealership looking for a car for her. After a while, she stopped next to a bright red Mustang.

This was not just any ordinary Mustang. It was a Termi-nator. Ford threw down the gauntlet in the early 2000's with their Cobra Mustang. It was the most powerful muscle car you could buy. It was so powerful that consumers soon nicknamed them Terminators. The name stuck.

The salesman ran inside to grab the keys. He came out with a big smile and a pair of Oakley sunglasses on. He was about to go on a test drive with a beautiful blonde in an awesome convertible on a perfect spring day. Life was good.

---

18 You don't need a driver's license to buy or finance a car. About 1/3 of our customers don't!

19 It's actually illegal to discuss pricing or terms with a minor.

20 More than one salesman has ended up in a trunk or kicked out when the vehicle was being stolen.

Like the cool guy he was, he tossed the blonde the keys and hopped into the passenger seat. He leaned back and put his feet up on the dash. She also got in the car and was smiling too. She started the car, a huge roar announced to us all that the Terminator was awake. She pulled the car out of its spot and crept to the exit of the dealership. We were on a pretty busy road and today was no exception.

After waiting a while, she saw a gap and punched the gas. I'm guessing this was her first time driving a car with enough power to rotate the earth. The car roared and surged into traffic. She cranked the wheel and the car spun, howling in a cloud of smoke right into a telephone pole. Bam! We run over to the car as fast as we can. The girl is dazed but perfectly okay, not even a scratch. The salesman on the other hand was screaming and holding his hands between his legs. In his attempt to look cool, he had put his feet on the dash so when the airbag deployed, it hit him right in his groin area. It hit him so hard that he broke his pelvis. When the police arrived, they ticketed the girl. It turned out that the girl was 17. This meant that the insurance company would not cover the accident or his injuries. In the end, the salesman got fired and got a pelvis cast. The girl and I got an exciting story.

CHAPTER 2:

The Process

The sales process is beaten into every car salesperson's head from day one. Woe to the salesperson whose manager finds out a step was skipped.

To almost every customer, this is a seamless process. To the minority, it is an annoyance slowing them down from their true goal of "just give me your best price."

The basic process has 6 steps: the greeting, interview, landing on a car, walk-around, test drive, and finally the negotiation. Why all these steps and can we just skip to the chase? Well, the reason for the steps is a long perfected dance to lead to maximum sales. As to if you can skip it, the answer is sometimes but it is rarely in your favor to do so.

We are going to go into more detail on the individual steps, why they happen and how to use them to your advantage. When you understand the steps, you will also understand why you shouldn't try and skip them.

Step 1: The Greeting

This is a necessary first step, not so much to sell a car, but because society dictates it. A greeting starts when you first talk to your salesperson. The salesperson is said to be "upping" you at this point. Some greetings are scripted, some are not.

Basically, it's just a quick introduction of everybody to break the ice. It usually lasts less than a minute and leads into...

Step 2: The Interview

This step lays the foundation of everything to come. It is the step where the salesperson tries to deduce your wants and needs.

It usually starts with a question along the lines of "What can I help you folks find today?" To which the average customer answers, "we're just looking." This is one of the first mistakes customers make, not trying to utilize the salesperson from the start.

There are a few things you need to understand about salespeople, how they are managed and how they are paid. First, any salesperson that just says "Okay" to your claim of "I'm just looking" and walks away is out of a job. Second, the salesperson only makes money if you buy a car and he has very little control over the profit, which is the sales manager's job.

When you say I'm just looking, the salesperson will reply with a glib line and a smile. "Wonderful, what are we looking for?" This leads to an awkward moment as you realize the salesperson isn't going anywhere.

When I say that salespeople have very little control over the profit, it's basically because they don't care. Almost all new car sales are called "minis". That means the salesperson makes a minimum commission, usually around 200-300 dollars. This is because there is so little markup in most cars that almost all deals lose money before dealer bonuses get figured in. Typical dealer bonuses of a few hundred dollars don't get paid out to the salespeople. On top of that, the dealership usually gives bonuses to salespeople at certain volume goals. What this means is that the typical salesperson doesn't care what car you buy, how much your trade is worth or how much you pay, just that you buy.

How does this affect you? Basically, you're stuck with dealing with the salesperson. You want to buy a car at a great price. He wants to sell a car at any price. This is a match made in heaven.

How do you use this to your advantage? Get the salesperson on your side. Instead of having to infer what you want, be open and direct. The better picture the salesperson has of what it will take to sell you a car, the easier everything will be.

With that in mind, how should you respond to his question of "How can I help you folks today?" Something like this, "Well, we have a 4 year old Civic we need to trade in for a minivan. We've decided we want a 2020 Dodge Caravan LE. Could you show us which one you think is the best deal? We are very payment conscious."

This stops the salesperson from trying to open a clam to get information and puts the salesperson firmly on your team. How? Well for one, you've stated you're a serious buyer, and with only 1 in 5 customers buying[21], that separates you from the pack. Second, you know what you want and now so does the salesperson. The only thought now is which one is the best deal[22]. At the beginning of the book, I discussed the power of being a nice, normal person. This is where that starts.

Step 3: Landing

Once the interview is complete, the salesperson's goal is to "land" you on a vehicle. "Land" is an industry term that means you have picked out a car. This is where your pre-purchase homework comes into play.

A car dealership is an adult's toy store. As you're headed back to the minivan section, you're going to pass a lot of shiny vehicles you would probably rather own. It is your job to stay focused on your end goal, the vehicle you pre-picked and re-searched. I can't overstate this piece of advice not staying focused on the car you chose in the first place is the biggest mistake consumers make.

Getting a great deal on a car you just saw, without research "in the ether[23]" as it's called, takes skill and emotional control

---

21 A 20% closing ratio (1 in 5) is considered industry standard.

22 How can different new cars of the same model be deals? There are many reasons why 2 similar new cars can be bought for more or less. Sometimes there are dealer demos. New car owners/managers put 1000 miles or so on it and these are sold at discounts. Sometimes the dealer is extra motivated to move certain colors or trims if they have excess.

23 Customers who fall in love with a car are said to be in the ether. A common statement the day after is "Mr. Jones just called; he fell out of the ether." Oops, reality must have set in.

that few people have. If you do find yourself interested in a different car, leave. Come back tomorrow AFTER you have done all your homework over.

If you continue down the sales process (I just want to see what it drives like, well it couldn't hurt to see the numbers, etc.), you're going to have a bad day. And for God's sake, do not let the salesperson talk you into taking the car when you leave as an extended test drive. This is called the puppy dog close, based on how effective puppy sales tactics are. "Well Mr. Smith, just take the puppy home, if your wife or kids don't want it, just bring it back." This close has been used as long as puppies have existed. Puppies returned to date: 0.

Okay, you've remained strong and the salesperson has shown you a vehicle that is a good deal. It's the vehicle you've researched and you like it.

Step 4: The Walk-around

The walk-around starts with the salesperson pulling the vehicle out of an unending row of similar vehicles. He then butterflies[24] the vehicle and proceeds to tell you about certain features and demonstrates how different things work.

While this step seems simple enough, it is actually very important and powerful. By pulling the car away from its nearly identical sisters, it isolates the car and makes it unique. This car, subconsciously, starts becoming your car.

---

24 This is when the hood, truck and all of the doors are opened to facilitate the salesperson showing you the vehicle.

You must dodge this mental trap when the negotiation begins. It is not unique, there are many just like it, probably on that very lot. If you start getting attached, it will cost you.

This is the most scripted part of a salesperson's job. There are even national walk-around contests by the various manufacturers. They usually start at the hood, rotate to the passenger side, then rear, ending at the driver's door. The salesperson will then ask you to sit down and see how it "feels". Knowing it or not, you have now begun the next step.

Step 5: The Test Drive

Getting a customer on a test drive is a mile marker for a salesperson. Most salespeople are judged on three numbers: the number of ups they've had (customers), number of test drives and the number of sales. Once you go on a test drive, the chance you become a sale has gone from 20% to 50%[25].

The test drive itself is very important for you. It also happens to be the step people wish to skip the most. Don't skip it. We discussed that you going on a test drive increases the probability for a sale. That also means the manager (who dictates the price) is much more interested and motivated by a customer that has gone on a test drive. They consider it "skin in the game," meaning that you have committed your time to drive the car, so you must be serious. Plus, every manager has taken the time to negotiate a deal with a customer who hasn't

_____
25 We discussed that 1 in 5 customers buy (20%) but it's also true that on average 1 in 2 buy that test drive (50%).

driven the vehicle only to find out afterwards that the seat hurt the customer's back. This is a lesson for the manager not soon forgotten.

Most dealerships have a pre-planned route they prefer you to take. There are a few reasons for this. For one, if you run out of gas[26], they know where to find you. The next 2 reasons are not so much in your favor. The route is usually on ideal roads that minimize any road noise or harshness. This can blanket issues of unusual sounds or vibration that could annoy you later. The scariest reason is that the salesperson is giving you directions on where to go. This pre-programs you to following the salesperson's direction, not just driving. Many studies have been done on this specific subject[27]. Because of these facts; many salespeople are trained to climb the "yes ladder" with customers. Do you like how that seat feels? Yes. Do you like this car's interior? Yes.

To avoid these subconscious manipulations, avoid the dealer's route. Tell the salesperson you want to see what it drives like on certain roads or on the freeway. The salesperson will comply with your request, because these manipulations are beyond most salespeople's perspectives. They know they get in trouble if they don't do certain things but often don't know the reason. As you drive the vehicle, ignore the new car euphoria. Do you like the way it drives? Is it comfortable? These are the questions you focus on.

---

26 This happens a shocking number of times

27 Some of my favorite books on the subject are "Influence" and "Pre-Suasion" both by Robert Cialdini, a behavioral psychologist.

As your test drive ends, you will come back to the dealership. The salesperson will ask you to park next to your trade, assuming you have one. This is yet another ploy to make the negotiations easier for the dealer. Not only are you still following orders, you're pulling "your" bright, shiny, new car next to your old, dirty car. You being able to compare the two next to each other is a very powerful weapon for the dealership.

After parking, the salesperson will say something like, "Okay, let's go inside and look at some numbers." Again, this is predisposing you to follow orders. He cleverly avoids the mention of buying the car and instead says you're only going to "look at some numbers[28]."

Before getting too upset by these manipulations, understand they are not meant for you. They are for an uninformed buyer that must be coaxed and herded through the sales process. So smile, take it in stride and admire the game for what it is. Remember, most of these tricks only work subconsciously. By being aware, you are immune.

Step 5.5: The Trade

This is the middle step if you have a trade. It's not a step that is really taught to salespeople so I don't want to claim it as part of the sales process, but your trade would come up here chronologically.

---

28 Even though a customer is obviously at a dealership to buy a car, the mere mention of actually buying a car will send most customers running, so smart dealers will avoid any word that actually reflects a purchase being made.

A trade appraisal is made on every possible trade in. Things like miles, condition and trim options go on here. Usually it starts with the salesperson or used car manager asking you to show them your car. Even when the request is not made, the customer will still be asked for their keys so the manager can look at the vehicle. This invariably leads to the customer going outside anyways to watch.

The used car manager will slowly walk around the vehicle. On his route, he will touch every ding, caress every scratch and lightly pick at every chip. This action will lead to a customer hastily explaining away the blemishes, while also subconsciously lowering the value of the car. The manager will scoff, "Don't worry, that's easy to fix, but the damage has been done."

Don't get upset. You have to understand both sides of the coin. As a dealer, I think I have better odds of hitting the Powerball lottery than a customer actually knowing what their trade is worth. These consistent and unrealistic expectations force games like these to be played.

What should you do instead? First and most important, heed the information in Part 2, Chapter 5 and know what your car is worth. Second, toss the dealer the keys, stay inside and enjoy the complimentary donuts and coffee while they appraise your trade.

Step 6: Negotiation

This is where the rubber meets the road. Do well on this step and you will probably save more money over your buying lifetime than you make in a year. Do bad... well, someone's got to pay to keep the dealer's lights on.

This is the most important step, so important I dedicated the entire next chapter to it. Just remember to prepare first! Follow the advice up until now and this will be much easier for you.

Funny but true

I doubt most consumers know this, but when you have your credit run by a car dealer, they run you against a terrorist watch-list too. It's automatic and it's called an OFAC check.

I've personally run thousands of credit reports and never seen anything but a clear OFAC message at the top of the credit report. Nobody I know even talks about it, it's almost invisible because everyone comes back "OFAC OK".

One day I was running the credit for a customer. When the credit popped up, instead of the ubiquitous "OFAC OK" message, it immediately announced that there was a match on the watch-list. "Warning: This individual may be dangerous and is on a federal watch-list. Do not give any indications to the individual in question; it may cause a dangerous situation." I became very nervous. The final message was a request to call the FBI at its 24-hour emergency terrorist response hotline with instructions to make this call from a secure location.

I calmly meander to a back office and proceed to freak out. I lock the door, hide behind a desk and dial the number. It answers "You have called the FBI's terrorist response hotline. If you have a positive hit on an OFAC report, press 1." I quickly press the 1 button. "If the individual in question is still at your location, press 1." I jam the 1 button. It reads me the same riot act that was on the credit report and hypes me up with images of men in black helicopters kicking in the windows to snatch this guy.

It then says it will transfer me to an agent. It rings and rings and finally picks up. A pre-recorded message comes on, "Please leave a message after the beep... Beeep!" What the heck?! I have a deadly super terrorist here! A message, fine!

I leave the message with all of the details including his description, what kind of car he wanted, the fact that my credit company said that he was a terrorist. I gave so much information that the answering machine cut me off.

Not knowing what else to do, I went back to my desk. I told the salesperson that his customer couldn't buy and let him leave. I got his license plate number and pulled all of the surveillance video on the guy. I figured I might as well be ready when the feds come in.

But they didn't come in and never called me back! I had left 4 messages, sent a few e-mails and felt I did my civic duty.

That was roughly 9 years ago. I still haven't heard anything from the FBI, but I've still got that video, just in case.

CHAPTER 3:

The Negotiation

Well, it all comes down to this. The part most people dread. But worry not, if you've followed my advice before arriving at this point, you are doing well. Assuming you follow through on what this chapter teaches you, you're guaranteed to end up with a great deal.

Now before we go into the trenches, you need a couple of tools. First, you will need a financial calculator. Years ago this was almost unheard of, today though you can download one of hundreds on your phone for free. Second, you will need all of your research before going into the dealership. Now, you're ready.

It all starts with the pencil. No, not the old graphite #2 pencil you remember from grade school. A pencil is what dealers call the paper they present you with all of the numbers on it. The first iteration you see is a "first pencil" and each one after that is one number higher i.e. a second or third pencil.

The belief is that a customer who agrees to the first pencil is a lay down[29] and a customer who needs 4 or 5 pencils to close is a pain. Everyone else lands on a spectrum between

---

29 Basically, a sucker

those extremes. A pencil is delivered on a piece of paper that looks like this:

Customer info	
Trade	Purchase Vehicle
2001 Honda Accord $3,500	2020 Nissan Altima $27,995
Down	Payment
$2,500↓	@ 629.14 mo

For this example, we are assuming a purchase not a lease.

This form is called a "4-square" for obvious reasons. This simplifies the deal and breaks it into four easily understood quadrants. However, this form is not designed this way for ease; it is designed this way for dealer profits.

Even though at first blush, it seems to disclose much, it really shows you nothing but your trade value. The price was already on the side of the car and the down payment and monthly payment are exaggerated to get you focused on them. The hope is that you negotiate those two boxes and ignore the other two "God Boxes". They are called that because nobody but God should lower them (in the dealer's eyes).

What you need to pay attention to is what the four-square doesn't show. There are no rebates listed, no interest rate, not even the payment term! Its sole purpose is to have you jump up and down and exclaim how ridiculous the payment is. The salesperson would then calmly explain that it was figured at only 48 months and would ask what kind of payment you were looking for. You have now been diverted from the top two boxes showing the trade value and price.

But you dear reader are no average customer. You are prepared! You know what the payment should be, your trade value (roughly) and you will not be phased by the first pencil. So what should you do? Relax, smile and calmly ask for the invoice or book sheet on the car you are trying to buy, the book sheet on your trade and the ACV. ACV stands for Actual Cash Value and it's the true value they are putting on your car.

Politely tell them the numbers you are willing to pay, or be paid in the case of your trade. Do not allow the conversation for payment or down payment to happen until these matters are settled.

Once those numbers are agreed to and only then can you talk about payment and down payment. Disclose what rate you found and tell them you are okay with the dealer financing the vehicle if they can meet or beat that rate.

You have now negotiated a great price on your car, but unbeknownst to most customers, the negotiation isn't over!

The Hidden Negotiation

After you agree to your deal, it's time to go to the finance department. The finance office is where most consumers blow their deal. Most people assume you're just going to sign paperwork but that is just the wrapping paper. The finance department on average makes more money on a car than the sales department makes on the sales price of the car.

What the finance department is really trying to do is sell you products like warranties and gap insurance. Let's look at some of these products.

Extended warranty

An extended warranty can be sold on both a new and a used vehicle. Unless you're the kind of person that keeps a car forever, I'd skip it on a brand new vehicle.

On a used vehicle it can make sense. The prices vary greatly depending on the car and how long you are protected. I do suggest always getting the highest level coverage of the warranty; the lesser ones exclude things and that will inevitably be the thing that breaks.

GAP insurance

If you are in an accident and your vehicle is totaled, your insurance company will pay the value of the vehicle at the time of the accident. GAP would pay the difference or "gap".

If you put no down or a little down, traded in a vehicle with negative equity, this is a must. Financing for extended terms (longer than 48 months) also increases the chance of having a gap when the car is totaled.

Basically if you put 20% down or more, don't worry too much about it. Otherwise, I'd recommend getting it.

Life and Disability Insurance

The industry term is LaHa and you can also purchase this while financing the vehicle. The idea is that in the event of your death or disability, the car will be paid for.

My recommendation is a hard pass. You can buy the same policy amount from a life insurance company for a fraction of the price.

VTR or Etch

VTR stands for Vehicle Theft Registration. It's also called Etch because it's an option to etch the glass of the car with your VIN. There is usually some small cash insurance policy if the vehicle is stolen and not recovered.

While this is a real product and very common, it leans into scam territory. VRT usually costs the dealer $20 and they sell it for any price they want, I've seen it as high as $3,000! This is one to avoid at all costs.

Tire and Wheel

This one is pretty straightforward. Tire and Wheel covers the replacement cost of either the tires or wheels of the vehicle if they get damaged. On most vehicles, I would pass.

The answer is maybe if you are buying a high performance vehicle, like a Corvette or a Porsche. A wheel or tire on these cars can be very expensive. With individual tires costing $1,000 and wheels sometimes tripling that amount, it might not be a bad idea. Weigh the trade-offs based on your driving habits.

Anything Else

There are packages for scotch-guarding your interior, undercoating your car, ceramic coating your exterior, etc. Avoid them all. They are pure profit centers and add little if any value to your car.

The way the finance office works is pretty much the same everywhere. They will have you verify your information and start signing forms. Then they will pull out a menu that looks something like this:

Mr. & Mrs. Jones 2020 Honda Civic 60x279			
Bronze	Silver	Gold	Platinum
60x299	66x299	72x299	72x319
10 years	10 years	10 years	10 years
100k warranty	100k warranty	100k warranty	100k Warranty
	Gap	Gap	Gap
		Wheel & Tire	Wheel & Tire
		LA/H	LA/H
X_____	X_____	X_____	Protection Package
			X_____

They will then pitch the various products. If any appeal to you, discuss them. Understand that you are not obligated to buy any of the packages as they are offered. You can pick any one, two or even none of the items.

WHY BUYING A CAR SUCKS

Do not be pressured into buying something you do not want. The finance people are by far the best quality and highest producing salespeople in the dealership. Be warned.

Once the sales portion of the finance process is over, you will then sign the contract. Do not rush this! Slowly verify all of the numbers down the contract. Check to make sure the price, term, interest rate and payment are all correct.

Unscrupulous dealers and/or finance people can do what's called payment packing. This is basically quoting you a payment higher than what the real numbers reflect. They do this to include back end products. This means you must look over every line of a contract!

After all this... you just bought a car! Not only did you buy one, you got a deal not many others are capable of negotiating. As long as you always do your homework, control your emotions and pay attention to the numbers, you will always end up with a great deal! Congrats!

Funny but True

Most dealerships use some kind of a voucher system to get gas. The salesperson will fill out a voucher, have it signed and then give it to someone at the gas station. This is used to reduce theft. Usually a car only needs gas once or twice, but sometimes older vehicles need gas 3 or more times.

One day, our office manager came to me with a stack of vouchers. One vehicle had been filled with gas 15 times! The vehicle was a new, large SUV. It was an old car, but not old enough to need a fill up 15 times. She couldn't figure out how it was possible, and neither could I at first.

I went to go look for the vehicle and couldn't find it. It should have been up front with the other SUVs but it wasn't. I sent the lot porters to search for it. We had over 800 vehicles so it was a bit like looking for a needle in a haystack.

It was finally found buried deep in the back lot. The lot porter told me I had to come see it. I went on a short hike to the vehicle. It was in the farthest back corner possible. I looked inside and was shocked, it was full of stuff. There was a TV, sleeping bag, clothes and food all set up like a tent. Someone had been living in the truck!

We went to the video surveillance to try and figure out what was going on. We went to the night before and saw a salesman go to the vehicle and get in it after we closed. He was in there the whole night. We fast forwarded to morning and he got out about an hour before we opened.

We tried to figure out how long this had been going on for. We rewound it farther and farther back. Our hard drive only went back about 60 days and there he was living in it!

Somehow we had missed this. He had been living in an SUV for months! He would run the A/C all night and refill the gas when it got low. We were all stunned. The salesman made good money. Why was he doing this? We called him in to confront him with our knowledge and to find out why.

Apparently, his girlfriend had kicked him out and he had no money at the time. He decided to just sleep in a car and figure it out the next day. I asked him why he didn't get a place when he got paid. According to him, he was just too depressed to go look for one. Needless to say, he was fired. God only knows how long he could have done that if he had paid for his own gas.

Bonus Section

Buying a car with bad credit

Intro

Bad credit makes buying a car, which is already an unpleasant experience for some, into a total nightmare for some people. It makes everything harder all around. Insurance is more expensive, rental homes are hard to find, and even utility companies want their pound of flesh.

If you don't have bad credit, you may be quick to judge and think that people may deserve their credit. While I agree that typically people deserve their credit score, I don't agree that someone should be humiliated or degraded for it.

I've seen victims of domestic abuse, women who have lost young children, seniors whose life savings evaporated in the housing crash, divorces, and countless others put in positions that damaged or destroyed their credit.

How have I seen all of these people? I own a chain of car dealerships in Las Vegas[30] that deals exclusively with people who have bad credit. We are by far the highest volume subprime[31] dealer in Las Vegas. We sometimes see more customers in a day than our competitors will see in a month.

---

30 QueenMotorcars.com if you're interested

31 The polite way of saying bad credit

This has given me a unique perspective and I'm going to use that perspective to give anyone in that situation advice to get a car without getting ripped off.

CHAPTER 1:

Before you go to a dealer

The first thing any dealer is going to ask you for is "stips". Stips, short for stipulations, is proof of the things you claim on your application. Stips consist of a paystub, utility bill and references.

The paystub is the most common proof of income, also called POI. Any proof will work such as an SSI award letter and a few months of bank statements. We even have banks accepting PayPal deposits. Usually, you need your last two paystubs if you just started or when the new calendar year begins and your year to date (YTD) income starts over. If it's bank deposits, 3 months of statements will suffice.

A utility bill is a form of POR or proof of residence. Your most recent power bill will have your name and address on it and will have been mailed to you within the last 30 days. Some banks will not accept a bill if it has an outstanding balance (a payment past due), so try to bring one that doesn't. If you can't provide a bill with your name and address on it, a recent bank statement or a few pieces of junk mail should do.

The last thing the dealer will need is a list of references, usually 4-8. A reference is the name, phone number, address and relation of someone you know.

Don't make the mistake of trying to falsify stips. Both the dealer and the bank will catch it. You're much better off being honest. They can't make money if they don't sell you a car. There are legit ways around everything!

With these 3 documents, you are ready to find a dealer, but which one?

CHAPTER 2:

Find a Dealer

This is probably the most important thing when buying a car with bad credit. Not all dealers are created equal when it comes to financing someone with bad credit. There are two main types of subprime dealers.

Buy here pay here (BHPH)

These dealers are their own bank. They finance the cars themselves. They are fairly easy to spot they announce things like "no credit check" or "your job is your credit".

Dealers who finance through lending institutions

These dealers finance you through a multitude of banks, private lenders and credit unions. They are harder to spot but you usually find much nicer and newer cars there.

So which is right for you? Almost always, it is the more traditional dealer that finances through lending institutions. There are several reasons why these dealers are better for the consumer. I'll go over some of the major ones.

Traditional dealers have access to hundreds of different lending sources, so they can actually finance worse credit.

People mistakenly believe that BHPH dealers finance worse credit, but it's not true. A BHPH dealer is risking their own money so they are more conservative. Plus, it's only one person. If they say no, it's a no. Traditional dealers use other people's money and if one says no, there are dozens of others.

Another huge difference is the vehicles for sale. A BHPH dealer is their own bank. Salvage, TMU[32], and all other similar types of vehicles are common because they are cheaper to buy. A traditional dealer has to sell his loan off to an investor. That means no salvage, no odometer issues and no lemon law cars. Since BHPH dealers use their own money they are usually buying $1,000-3,000 cars. Because of the investors they have to sell the loan to, traditional dealers have much newer and nicer cars.

The down payments and monthly payments are a huge difference as well. BHPH usually tries to get a down payment large enough to cover the purchase price of the vehicle! That's right; they want $2,500 down on the car they bought for $2,500! They also want large payments every 2 weeks. Traditional dealers don't care too much about the down payment. Because the bank finances the rest, you also get a smaller monthly payment!

So basically, a traditional dealer has nicer and newer cars, lower payments, down payments, and interest rates. Besides that, they can finance people with credit issues exceeding what BHPH dealers can handle. It's a black and white choice.

---

32 True mileage unknown, basically the odometer is broken

The question is how do you know which is which? Just ask. A BHPH dealer brags about "in-house financing". They won't deny it. A traditional dealer will tell you they finance through lending institutions[33]. It's that easy.

Now you know which kind of dealer to go to and how to identify them. Are there any downsides to traditional financing? Because a traditional dealer might shop your application to dozens of different lenders, it can take several hours to get approved. However, most would agree that it's a small price to pay for all the benefits you get in return.

So which traditional dealer do you go to? I find that online reviews are the most reliable indicator. Go to a dealer with a high volume of positive reviews for best results.

---

33 Sometimes a traditional dealer will say both. That's usually so they don't scare away any customers who think their credit is too bad for normal financing.

CHAPTER 3:

The Car

Typically, once you get in the subprime market, the dealer will get you approved first and then show you the cars that work for that approval. Take your time and look over the car well. The individual policies of the lenders will protect you from the worst issues, like savage vehicles, but the rest is up to you.

Make sure there are no metal on metal noises from the engine or when you drive it. Does the transmission shift normally? Does everything work?

Sometimes you don't have a lot of choices when buying subprime, but you always have the choice to leave.

CHAPTER 4:

Putting It All Together

Compared to buying a new car with good credit, buying a car with bad credit is actually simpler. It's not as easy, but less complex.

As long as you take the time to get your stips in order before you go to the dealership, pick the correct type of dealer and pick a decent car, you will be fine.

My last piece of advice is to not give up. Our average customer has been turned down by 4 different dealerships before we sell them a car! I wish I could tell the people that give up after one or two attempts this piece of information.

Appendix

APPENDIX A:

Tips, Tricks and General Advice

There are a few things I'd like to go over with you that don't fit anywhere else. The first is about buying a car in general.

Basically, people buy cars above their means. With low interest rates, insanely long terms, leases and low down payments, people can buy much more car than they should.

The 24/7 rule of thumb most financial advisors quote is fairly easy to remember. 24/7 breaks into 3 numbers: 20, 4 and 7. The rule is to put at least 20% down, for a maximum of a 4-year payment and up to 7% of your net income towards that payment.

Banks will allow up to 20% of your monthly gross income to go to a car payment with no money down and up to 120 months! But just because they allow it, doesn't make it a good idea. Let's now move into some tips and tricks.

Extra Payments

Like a mortgage, interest is front loaded on a car loan. Making extra payments towards the principal of the loan can save you loads of interest, especially in the beginning. This is particularly powerful if you are at a high interest rate.

Ethical Bribes

When negotiating for a car (especially a new car), try an ethical bribe. Promise and follow through with a great online review and a perfect 10 on the customer satisfaction survey. This is super important to dealers and might turn a no into a yes!

GAP Insurance

If you're buying a vehicle and need GAP insurance, call your insurance agency first. Many offer it at a cheaper price.

Extended Warranty

Did you know that you don't need to buy an extended warranty at the time of purchase? You can always come in later and buy one. Just make sure your factory warranty is still active or it gets more expensive.

If you do buy a warranty, make sure it is a factory warranty. Some dealers sell their own brand for extra profit. The factory one is better.

Buy On Slow Days

Most customers buy a car on a weekend or holiday weekend. For the best deals and a quicker process, show up on a Tuesday night. It's usually the slowest day of the week.

Buy Only in One Person's Name

If your credit and income will allow it, never put your spouse on a car loan, credit cards, house, etc. The co-signor is equally responsible for the loan. If something happens in life and you have to go bankrupt, leaving your spouse off of the loan will preserve that person's credit.

Always Cancel the Back End

Backend products like warranty and gap are cancelable. Make sure you cancel them when you trade your car in and get the money back. 99% of consumers don't do this!

Negotiate Online First

If you're not confident in your ability to negotiate, do it online first. This is a great way to lock in the numbers before you show up.

APPENDIX B:

The Truth about Consumer Advocacy Companies

With so many companies out there "helping" people buy cars, why has nothing changed? I hate to be the one telling you this, but it's because they don't want it to.

Ask yourself this question. How does Yelp, TrueCar, CarFax and others make money? They have to make it somewhere and their ads are constantly on National TV campaigns.

The answer is that they charge dealers. The CarFax ads imply that if the dealer doesn't give it to you, they are shady and hiding something. Or, maybe they don't want to pay the $39 it costs per CarFax. Don't believe me? Go to CarFax and try to pull one yourself.

What about TrueCar, Kelley Blue Book and Costco? They all advertise to get you the best price on a vehicle, but how? And how do they make money? Again, it's from the dealer. They are really just selling your lead to the dealer for $500-$700! You can easily get a better price without their "help" because the dealer doesn't have to pay for the lead!

How about Yelp? You guessed it. They get people with businesses to advertise with them for $700 a month... each. What do the businesses get for $700? They get almost nothing. Yet if you don't pay, your good reviews mysteriously become un-recommended and don't show up in the normal spots. There are multiple class action suits claiming just this. As a personal testament, my dealerships have almost a thousand good reviews on Google. There are 2 on Yelp. If you look deeper, there are over 300 5-star reviews that are not recommended. Maybe one day, I'll break down and pay the $700, but not today.

What about our old standby, the Better Business Bureau? The name sounds like some government entity but it's not. It's a for profit business that charges other businesses to make money. They charge a business to become a BBB member and once you're a member, it's almost impossible to lose your A+ rating.

The moral of this story is to not place your trust into any 3rd part entity. Only you will have your best interest in mind. Act accordingly.

APPENDIX C:

Leases

L eases are fairly simple, but complicated jargon obscures them to where many people can't understand them. In its most basic form, a lease is just you paying the depreciation of the car and not the principal.

Think of an interest only loan on a home. Basically, they give you a percentage of the depreciation. If it's 30%, that is the amount you would end up paying for the car plus interest and profit. You can negotiate price and payments just like a normal car purchase.

❀
The Final Word

I hope this book has opened your eyes and answered a lot of questions for you. If it has helped you, I'd love to hear from you. You can e-mail me at queenmotorcars@gmail.com. Feel free to contact me with any additional questions you have as well.

For any consumers with bad credit, please consider my chain of used car dealerships in Las Vegas, NV.

Tina

www.ingramcontent.com/pod-product-compliance
Lightning Source LLC
Chambersburg PA
CBHW030847180526
45163CB00004B/1479